Excel
Basic Skills

Spelling and Vocabulary

5–6 Years

Ages 10–12

Peter Clutterbuck

Get the Results You Want!

PASCAL PRESS

Reprinted 1999, 2001, 2002, 2004, 2006, 2008, 2009, 2010, 2011 (twice), 2014, 2017, 2018, 2019, 2020, 2021, 2022, 2023, 2025

ISBN 978 1 86441 283 3

Pascal Press
PO Box 250
Glebe NSW 2037
www.pascalpress.com.au

Publisher: Vivienne Joannou
Typeset by Grizzly Graphics (Leanne Richters)
Cover by DiZign Pty Ltd
Printed by Vivar Printing/Green Giant Press

About this book

Excel *Basic Skills Spelling and Vocabulary* titles are designed not only to help children improve their spelling skills, but also to widen their knowledge of words.

The activities are simple and self-explanatory, allowing children to work independently within any particular area where they are experiencing difficulty. Answers are provided in a removable answer section.

The book contains all the elements of spelling and vocabulary relevant to Year 5 and Year 6. Parents and teachers will not only be able to direct children to specific activities for which there is a need, but will also obtain ideas for further activities to strengthen and reinforce needed skills.

TABLE OF CONTENTS

DOUBLE LETTERS

Double letters are an important part of many words. They often occur naturally but sometimes have to be added when we add endings.
For example, swim + ing = swimming

Example

Write the correct double letters in the space.
I put some bu_______er on my potato.
(rr tt ll)
*Answer = I put some bu**tt**er on my potato.*

Now do these the same way.

1. You need balls and a racquet to play te_____is.
(bb ll nn)

2. Bulls and cows are known as ca_______le.
(mm rr tt)

3. We put the ru_______ish in the bin.
(ff gg bb)

4. He tried to hit the ball but mi_______ed.
(mm ll ss)

5. We walked from the top to the bo_______om of the hill.
(ss tt pp)

6. The teacher gave us a le_______on about first aid.
(pp tt ss)

7. A colourful bird is a pa_______ot.
(pp ss rr)

8. Another name for noon is mi_______ay.
(dd ff ll)

9. My father works in a large o_______ice.
(pp ff cc)

10. The wine is kept in a wooden ba______el.
(rr mm pp)

11. We saw a po_______um in the tree.
(nn ss pp)

12. The baby wore a pretty bo_______et on her head.
(ss nn tt)

SILENT LETTERS

Silent letters were once sounded in the word. Although we no longer sound them, we have left them in the original word. For this reason they can cause spelling difficulties.

Example

Write the correct word and circle the silent letter.
A baby sheep is called a ____________.
(kitten lamb)
Answer = A baby sheep is called a ***lamb***

Now do these the same way.

1. I cut the meat with a ____________.
   (fork knife)

2. Jan threw the lolly ____________ in the bin.
   (wrapper milk)

3. We waited over an ____________ for him.
   (minute hour)

4. Mike brushed his hair with a ____________.
   (comb spoon)

5. A young cow is called a ____________.
   (calf puppy)

6. When he fell he hurt his ____________.
   (knee bike)

7. Sir Galahad put the ____________ back in its sheath.
   (sword book)

8. The greedy girl ate the ____________ cake.
   (fruit whole)

9. We watched the monkey ____________ the tree.
   (climb bite)

10. The king lives in the ____________ on top of the hill.
    (castle house)

11. A tall ____________ tree is growing in the yard.
    (gum palm)

12. I asked a ____________ to mend the leaking tap.
    (pilot plumber)

DEMON WORDS

Some words often cause us spelling difficulties. These can be classed as Demon Words.

Example

Write the correct spelling of the word in the space.
It is ___________ seven o'clock.
(allmost almost)

*Answer = It is **almost** seven o'clock.*

Now do these the same way.

1. Will is ___________ the first into the classroom.
(always allways)

2. We must wait here ___________ the rain stops.
(untill until)

3. Freya ___________ she would help me move the chairs.
(sed said)

4. I put some __________ in my cup of tea.
(suger sugar)

5. I can see Tim ___________ down the road.
(comeing coming)

6. We all thought it was a _________________ day.
(beautiful beautifull)

7. I sewed the button back on with some ___________.
(cotten cotton)

8. The prisoner tried to ___________ from the cell.
(excape escape)

9. What an ___________ looking model aeroplane.
(orful awful)

10. The shipwrecked sailors swam to the ___________ of the nearby island.
(safty safety)

11. The number after thirty-nine is ___________.
(fourty forty)

12. What is your ___________ to my question?
(answer anser)

LETTER PATTERNS

Knowing the different letter patterns that occur in words can be a useful way of remembering how to spell them.

Example

Circle the word which contains the same letter pattern as the bold word.
Write the pattern.
I had a quick ***snack*** *for lunch.*
(peach jacket lemon)
Answer = ***ack***

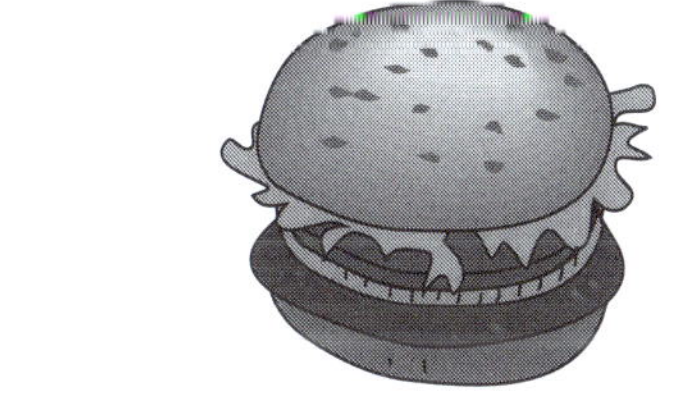

Now do these. Write the word on the line and circle the pattern.

1. The dog chased **after** the cat.
   (daily craft quack)

   ____

2. A palm tree is a large **plant**.
   (infant angle snake)

   ____

3. The **swallow** built a nest of mud and sticks.
   (bird allow feather)

   ____

4. I tried to **explain** the problem to her.
   (paint book teacher)

   ____

5. I sat on the old **armchair**.
   (table sofa repair)

   ____

6. The child ate all the **candy**.
   (wand lolly sweet)

   ____

7. I ate a **peach** for lunch.
   (apple teacher apricot)

   ____

8. The motorist put her foot on the **brake.**
   (lake car bonnet)

   ____

9. I hope I do not get the **blame.**
   (punish strap became)

   ____

10. There is a large **factory** on the corner.
    (tractor wool sheet)

    ____

11. We made toast out of the slices of **bread**.
    (ready drone peel)

    ____

12. David was so tired he fell **asleep** in class.
    (awake ready sweep)

    ____

UNIT 5 WORDS WE SOMETIMES CONFUSE Year 5

We often spell a word incorrectly because we confuse it with another word. This is particularly so for homophones (see Unit 21) and also for some other words.

Example

Write the correct word in the space.
Everyone ______________ Bill is allowed to come.
(accept except)
Answer = Everyone ***except*** *Bill is allowed to come.*

Now do these the same way.

1. The dog licked __________ paws.
(its it's)

2. The bottle is now __________ of water.
(full fool)

3. After tea we went for a ____________ along the street.
(work walk)

4. They __________ playing football when he broke his leg.
(where were)

5. Today is the eighth day __________ ___the month.
(of off)

6. Are you going __________ the party tonight?
(to two too)

7. Is that __________ bike on the lawn?
(you're your)

8. I ______________ my new bike to school to show my friends.
(bought brought)

9. The parents are going to __________ a baby boy.
(adapt adopt)

10. Be careful you do not __________ your wallet.
(lose loose)

11. I wrote about what happened in my __________.
(dairy diary)

12. Callan always __________ his best work at school.
(dose does doze)

UNIT 6 SYLLABLES Year 5

Every syllable contains a vowel sound. The vowels are a, e, i, o and u. Sometimes y is used as a vowel.

Rearrange the syllables and write the word in the space.
I like to do lots of physical ________________ at school.
(er ex cises)
Answer = I like to do lots of physical ***exercises*** *at school.*

Now do these the same way.

1. Mr Smith is a ________________.
(ter car pen)

2. I wear woollen ________________ to bed.
(py mas ja)

3. Look out, the mice are ______________!
(cap es ing)

4. You must be careful of ________________ electrical wires.
(head ver o)

5. The little kitten gave me a great deal of ________________.
(ment en joy)

6. The clown is going to ________________ the children.
(ter en tain)

7. I put the screws and bolts in the ________________.
(in cab et)

8. The new plants soon began to ________________ their leaves.
(op de vel)

9. After the long run we were ________________ to have a rest.
(per des ate)

10. Do you ________________ what she is saying?
(stand un der)

11. The fourth day of the week is ______________.
(Wed day nes)

12. Andrew was a good ________________ to me on the excursion.
(pan com ion)

INITIAL BLENDS

Many words we use begin with the same *initial* or starting blend of letters. It is important we know and recognise the letters that come together to make the initial sound of the word.

Write the initial blend in the space.
A _____arrow is a small bird.
(sl sp tr)
Answer = A ***sp****arrow is a small bird.*

Now do these the same way.

1. This knife is sharp but that one is _____unt.
(dr br bl)

2. My parrot wanted another ______acker.
(br cr cl)

3. A kitten is very ______ayful.
(br pl sc)

4. I scribbled in the book with a ______ayon.
(cr bl pr)

5. Last night I had a strange ______eam when I was sleeping.
(cr dr sc)

6. There is a nice cool ______eeze blowing.
(br bl dr)

7. Katy is ______ipping across the yard.
(sk br pl)

8. Sandpaper is rough, but glass is _____ooth.
(sm sp st)

9. The ______iest married the couple in the chapel.
(pl gr pr)

10. The ______umber mended the leaking tap.
(pr pl sc)

11. I helped the farmer ______ough the paddock.
(pl pr gr)

12. James has a ______acture in a bone of his left hand.
(fl fr br)

FINAL BLENDS

Many words we use end in the same groups of letters. These letter groups are called *final blends*. It is important we are familiar with these to help us spell them correctly.

Example

Write the correct final blend in the space.
The stockmen are going to bra______ the cattle.
(st nd mp)
*Answer = The stockmen are going to bra**nd** the cattle.*

Now do these the same way.

1. This chicken is now quite plu______.
(nd lt mp)

2. Do you know the resu_____of the match?
(nd lt sk)

3. Alice and I sit at the same de______.
(st sk pl)

4. Joanne was so upset she we______ all morning.
(st pt lt)

5. I threw the bread cru______ to the birds.
(st nd pt)

6. The la______ helped us see in the dark.
(mp nt st)

7. The puppy began to ye______.
(lp nt ct)

8. I got the answer corre______.
(st ct sk)

9. She gave me a gi______ for my birthday.
(st ft lt)

10. I wore a leather be______ around my waist.
(lt st nd)

11. Are you going to spe______ all your money now?
(nd st ft)

12. We are going to have to shi ______ that box as it is in the way.
(lt ct ft)

If we are to become good spellers we must know the different sounds made by individual letters or groups of letters.

Write the missing sound unit in the space.
A goanna is a large liz_____d.
(ue ar ea)
*Answer = A goanna is a large liz**ar**d.*

Now do these the same way.

1. The children were very n______sy when they were playing.
(ar oi ue)

2. An ______gle is a large bird of prey.
(oa ea oy)

3. I thought that was an ______ ful thing to do to him.
(or ow aw)

4. Are you r______dy to leave yet?
(ea ee oo)

5. I put the milk in the s______cer.
(or au ow)

6. A mirr______ is also called a looking glass.
(or ar ai)

7. We ate a roast turk______ for Christmas dinner.
(ay ey or)

8. A native Australian animal is the kangar______.
(oo oa ea)

9. The water was stored in a w______r.
(ie ei oa)

10. I helped Mr Jones cut his he______.
(dge ous the)

11. That is a very br______t light.
(igh ough dge)

12. Our newspaper is delivered d ______ly.
(or ai au)

SPELLING RULES 1

Knowing certain spelling rules can help us become better spellers. However, to any rule there are exceptions so you must be on the look-out for these.

Rule 1 **-i** before **-e** except after **-c** when the sound is ee.
For example, **niece** **piece** but **ceiling**

However, **science**, **height**, **foreign** because the sound is not **-ee**.
When the sound is **-ay**, words are usually spelt **-ei** as in **neighbour**.

Rule 2 There is only one word that ends in **full** and that is the word **full** itself — all the others are **-ful**, for example, **beautiful**.

Rule 3 When a word ends in **-y** it is usually changed to **-i** when we add a suffix such as **-ly**, **-ful**, **-ed**. For example, **beauty** = **beautiful**.
It is not changed if we add **-ing** or we would have criing.

Put the correct spelling of the word in the space.
I saw her in the __________ (field feild)
*Answer = I saw her in the **field**.*

Now do these the same way.

1. He is said to be the __________ of the tribe.
(chief cheif)

2. The __________ was arrested by the police.
(theif thief)

3. Patrick is my best __________.
(friend freind)

4. Would you like another __________ of pie?
(peice piece)

5. What is the __________ of that table?
(wieght weight)

6. I put a __________ of sugar in my tea.
(spoonfull spoonful)

7. The choir was singing __________.
(sweetly sweetily)

8. The children finished the work __________.
(easyly easily)

9. I am __________ his work.
(copiing copying)

10. The teacher spoke __________ to the rude boy.
(angrly angrily)

11. We are __________ to get there on time.
(hurrying hurriing)

12. He had a life full of __________.
(happyness happiness)

UNIT 11 SPELLING RULES 2 Year 5

Knowing certain spelling rules can help us become better spellers.

When a word ends in two consonants and we want to add **-ed** or **-ing** no letters are doubled. For example, **bang** becomes **banged** and **banging.**

When a word ends in a consonant with one vowel before it we double the last letter before adding **-ed** or **-ing**. For example, **beg** — becomes **begged** or **begging.**

When a word ends in a silent **-e** we drop the **-e** before adding **-ing**. For example, **shine** — **shining**. Exceptions include singeing, dyeing, canoeing, ageing.

If the suffix begins with a consonant the silent **-e** is usually retained.
For example, **care** — **careful**

Example

Write the correct spelling.
Ian is ______________ the wood. (choping chopping)
Answer = Ian is ***chopping*** *the wood.*

Now do these the same way.

1. The store was ______________ last night.
(robed robbed)

2. The children are ______________ a song.
(singging singing)

3. The car ______________ at the corner.
(stoped stopped)

4. I am ______________ the football match.
(watching watchhing)

5. The dog is ______________ the cat.
(chasing chaseing)

6. I am ______________ to my friends.
(waveing waving)

7. I am ______________ he will arrive soon.
(hopful hopeful)

8. Tommy is ______________ the cake.
(icing iceing)

9. The teacher is ____________ the cloth blue.
(dying dyeing)

10. I thought his work was quite ____________.
(hopless hopeless)

11. Billy is ______________ to fix his old bike.
(triing trying)

12. The bees are ______________ loudly.
(huming humming)

PLURALS 1

The word plural means more than one.

1. Most words simply add **-s** to form their plurals. For example, one **cat** — two **cats**
2. Words ending in **-ch, -s, -sh, -z** or **-x** add **-es** to make their plurals. For example, one **bush** — two **bushes**
3. Most words ending in **-o** add **-es** to make their plurals. For example, one **tomato** — two **tomatoes**.
   However some, like piano, kangaroo, bamboo, photo, boo, radio, banjo, just add **-s**.

Write the plural in the space.
There are three ______________ in this street. (church)
*Answer = There are three **churches** in this street.*

Now do these the same way.

1. There are lots of tall ______________ in this forest. (tree)
2. I saw two ______________ in our backyard. (fox)
3. The good fairy gave me three ______________. (wish)
4. I ate two ______________for my lunch. (peach)
5. The baker baked seven ______________ of bread. (batch)
6. We had to dig two ______________ around the tents. (ditch)
7. All the ______________ are on the table. (glass)
8. Mel has five new hair ______________. (brush)
9. There are seven ______________ on the kitchen table. (potato)
10. I took lots of ______________ on my trip. (photo)
11. There are lots of ______________ in Hawaii. (volcano)
12. We listened to the football on the two ______________. (radio)

Some more plurals are:

1. Words ending in **vowel-y**, simply add **-s**. For example, one **monkey** — two **monkeys**
2. Words ending in **consonant-y** , change the **-y** to **-i** and add **-es**. For example, one **fairy** — two **fairies**
3. Words ending in **-f**, change the **-f** to **-v** and add **-es**. For example, one **wolf** — two **wolves**.

   However, there are lots of exceptions. For example, one **chief** — two **chiefs**
4. Some words make their plurals by changing vowels or adding **-en**.

   For example, one **woman** — two **women** one **ox** — two **oxen**

Write the plural.
Melbourne and Sydney are large ______________. (city)
Answer = Melbourne and Sydney are large ***cities****.*

Now do these the same way.

1. I put all the ______________ in the box. (toy)
2. There are seven ______________ in the yard. (donkey)
3. Donna has two pet ______________. (pony)
4. When all the ______________ began crying I left the room. (baby)
5. I saw a cow with two ______________. (calf)
6. We swept up all the ______________ on the lawn. (leaf)
7. The mountaineer climbed the three ______________. (cliff)
8. I have three ______________ in my pocket. (handkerchief)
9. I put the cups on the two ______________. (shelf)
10. I had three ______________ extracted yesterday. (tooth)
11. The ______________ walked into the room. (man)
12. There were over two hundred ______________ at the disco. (child)

UNIT 14 PROOFREADING Year 5

It is important that we are able to recognise whether a word is spelt correctly by simply looking at it. Proof reading is an important skill.

Example

In the sentence there is a word spelt incorrectly. Write it correctly.
Bill did not come becorse he was ill. ______________
Answer = ***because***

Now do these.

1. An elephant is big but a mouse is littel.

____

2. I like to spread buter on my bread.

____

3. My muther works at a garage.

____

4. A ripe banana is usually yelow.

____

5. I fourgot to bring my books.

____

6. I like to go swiming in summer.

____

7. There is a large cherch on the corner.

____

8. My berthday is next week.

____

9. I put the marbles in my poket.

____

10. I arsked him if he would help me.

____

11. It is allmost eight o'clock.

____

12. There were a lot of peeple at the football.

____

PREFIXES

Prefixes are syllables added to the front of a base word. They are often used to change a word to its opposite meaning. When you add a prefix you do just that — no spelling changes are needed.

Example

Choose the correct prefix to make the word have an opposite meaning.
The story I heard is_______true. (in un il)
*Answer = The story I heard is **un**true.*

Now do these the same way.

1. Jack is a very _______**happy** person.
(un in non)

2. Koalas are _______**common** in this area.
(in dis un)

3. Stealing goods is _______**legal**.
(il im in)

4. Scott is going to _______**dress**.
(un in sub)

5. Matthew _______ **locked** the door.
(in un mis)

6. That rude girl is very _______**polite**.
(un im dis)

7. When it disappeared into the clouds the plane became _______**visible**.
(un in il)

8. Smoking cigarettes is an _______**healthy** thing to do.
(in im un)

9. We are at a great _______**advantage**.
(dis ir un)

10. I'm sure that person is quite _______**sane**.
(il in un)

11. Mr Smith is a very ______**patient** person.
(il im un)

12. That was a very ______**honest** thing to do.
(dis un in)

SUFFIXES

Suffixes are groups of letters added to the ends of base words to build new words.

Example

Add the correct suffix from the brackets to complete the word.
Katy is a good swim_______. (est mer)
*Answer = Katy is a good swim**mer.***

Now do these the same way.

1. I am going to **short**_______ the piece of string. (en or)

2. That was a very **enjoy**______ trip. (ible able)

3. Is that the **loud**_______ it will go? (est er)

4. Be **care**_______ of that snake! (ful ing)

5. My mother is a **teach**_______. (or er)

6. My friend has a serious **ill**_______. (ness ure)

7. We are **butter**_______ the scones. (ry ing)

8. We are going to **black**______ the cloth. (en er)

9. This is the **clean**_______ my room has ever been. (ful est)

10. We are **hope**_______ he will arrive soon. (ful en)

11. I put my woollen **jump**_______ on. (or er)

12. The bread was made at the **bake**_______. (ary ery) (Remember your spelling rules with this one!)

Example

Using the suffixes in the box, see how many new words you can build.

er	ing	ed
ful	able	est

Base word = play
Answer = player, playing, played, playful, playable.

Now try these.

er	ed	est
ent	ful	ing

1. great ______________________________
____

2. clean ______________________________
____

3. sweet ______________________________
____

4. seat ______________________________
____

5. present ______________________________
____

6. spoon ______________________________
____

ed	ing	er
ant	able	ful

7. flood ______________________________
____

8. fly ______________________________
____

9. grow ______________________________
____

10. kick ______________________________
____

11. inform ______________________________
____

12. dream ______________________________
____

BASE WORDS

From *base* words we can build other words by adding a *prefix* or a *suffix* or *both*. For example:

Base Word	Add Prefix	Add Suffix
lock	**un**lock	**un**lock**ed**
happy	**un**happy	**un**happ**iness**
appear	**dis**appear	**dis**appear**ed**

Write the **base** word from which the bold word comes.
There are a lot of goods still ***unclaimed.*** ______________
Answer = ***claim***

Now do these the same way.
Circle the suffix or prefix and write the base word on the line.

1. Billy is **swimming** across the pool.

   ____

2. These stones over here are still **uncrushed**.

   ____

3. Dave is **disliked** because he is selfish.

   ____

4. The boys had a **disagreement** over who owned the bike.

   ____

5. This drawing I am doing is still **unfinished.**

   ____

6. That was a very **enjoyable** day.

   ____

7. Eating too much fatty food is **unhealthy**.

   ____

8. The carpenters are **rebuilding** the house.

   ____

9. It is **unlikely** he will come at this late hour.

   ____

10. Ian is a very **uncomplaining** type of person.

    ____

11. The umpire **disallowed** the free kick.

    ____

12. The shopkeeper happily **refunded** the money.

    ____

It is important for us to recognise the letter pieces that make up a word.

Example

Join the letter pieces together to make words that match the sentence.
I filled a ________________ and a ________________ with water.
(bot buc tle ket)
Answer = I filled a ***bottle*** *and a* ***bucket*** *with water.*

Now do these.

1. I have a ________________
and a________________.
(kit rab ten bit)

2. My ________________ put the
________________ on the bed.
(er pil moth low)

3. It is cold in ________________
and warm in ________________ .
(sum ter win mer)

4. I ________________ to put a bandage
on my ________________.
(fin got for ger)

5. I saw a________________ and three
________________ at the zoo.
(ras zeb key mon)

6. The ________________ sewed a
________________ on her shirt.
(doc but tor ton)

7. I saw lots of ________________
at ________________.
(peo rch chu ple)

8. The children ran ________________
the ________________.
(cle cir und aro)

9. I ate some ________________
for ________________.
(ner din ese che)

10. The ________________
________________ over the fence.
(don jum ped key)

11. I stood in the ________________
of the ________________.
(are mid dle squ)

12. The ________________ are in the
________________.
(hor ble sta ses)

UNIT 20 ANAGRAMS Year 5

Anagrams are words we can make by rearranging the letters of another word.

Example

Rearrange the letters to make a word that fits the sentence.
John is the captain of our ________________.
(meat)
Answer = John is the captain of our ***team****.*

Now do these the same way.

1. John has a big ________________ on his forehead.
(plum)

2. A ________________ stung the girl on the finger.
(paws)

3. I put the lovely ________________ in the vase.
(sore)

4. Robyn and I walked down the dark ________________.
(lean)

5. I put the cereal in the ________________.
(blow)

6. Maria won the ________________ easily.
(care)

7. The farmer dug a hole for the fence ________________.
(stop)

8. The small mouse was caught in the ________________.
(part)

9. I just don't know ________________ he did that.
(who)

10. I put the knives and forks on the ________________.
(bleat)

11. We watched the soldiers ________________ along the street.
(charm)

12. This toy is made of stainless ________________.
(sleet)

HOMOPHONES

Homophones are words that sound the same but have different spellings and different meanings. For this reason it is important we know both the spelling and the meaning of these words.

Example

Write the correct word.
In the forest we saw a large brown ________________.
(bare bear)
Answer = In the forest we saw a large brown ***bear****.*

Now do these the same way.

1. At the creek I saw a black____________ bush.
(berry bury)

2. The dog tried to ____________ the bone in the backyard.
(berry bury)

3. The dogs followed the ____________ of the escaped prisoner.
(cent scent)

4. These plants have ____________ a lot since last winter.
(groan grown)

5. Nick should be here in half an ____________.
(our hour)

6. Anita and I shared ____________ lunch.
(our hour)

7. The teacher gave us a ________________ about road safety.
(lesson lessen)

8. This will ________________ our chances of having an accident.
(lesson lessen)

9. The hunter fired the gun but the bullet ________________ its target.
(missed mist)

10. It was hard to see the feral pig in the ________________.
(missed mist)

11. I bought myself a new ____________ of woollen socks.
(pear pare pair)

12. I began to ____________ the water into the bottle.
(pour pore poor)

ANTONYMS

Antonyms are words that have the opposite, or nearly the opposite, meaning.

Example

Choose the word with the opposite meaning.
*That knife is **sharp** but this one is ____________*
(old blunt new)
*Answer = That knife is sharp but this one is **blunt.***

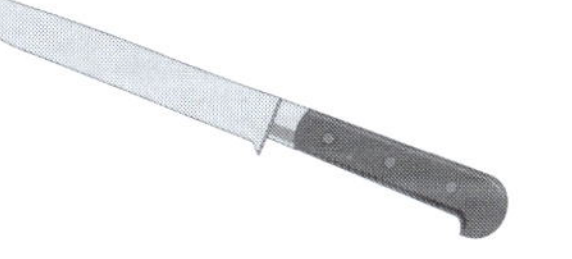

Now do these the same way.

1. Bill is **asleep** but Ned is already ____________.
(awake away eating)

2. Some children like to be **rough** when they play while others like to be ____________.
(silly clean gentle)

3. The puppies are **together** but the kittens are ____________.
(apart sleeping playing)

4. This bird is **thin** but that one is ____________.
(lean flying plump)

5. Josh will **accept** his present but Nguyen will ____________his.
(keep refuse open)

6. Mel likes to **save** her money while Bill likes to ____________ his.
(collect lose spend)

7. Those clothes are **spotless** but these are ____________.
(clean blue filthy)

8. My new toy can go **forwards** and also ____________.
(backwards fast slow)

9. The **inner** parts of the house are neat but the ____________ need a lot of work.
(inside outer roof)

10. I went **south** but the others began to walk ____________.
(west east north)

11. Michelle has a **smile** on her face, but Paul wears a ____________.
(grin frown scar)

12. That light is **strong** but this one is ____________.
(old bright feeble)

SYNONYMS

Synonyms are words that have the same, or nearly the same, meaning.

Circle the word that has the same meaning as the bold word.
*My parents said they would **let** me go to the disco.*
(help allow aloud)
*Answer = **allow***

Now, circle the word which has the same, or nearly the same, meaning.

1. It is silly to **boast** about the things you do.
(hate brag shout)

2. Right here the river is very **wide**.
(narrow broad fast)

3. A deer is a **swift** runner.
(slow fast silent)

4. Be careful you do not **bump** the table.
(rock discover knock)

5. I **possess** a new red bicycle.
(own found want)

6. The **rubbish** was put in the bin.
(food garbage rags)

7. I stood on the **edge** of the lawn.
(border centre side)

8. It was so cold we enjoyed the **heat** from the fire.
(flames coals warmth)

9. The stale food soon began to **rot**.
(decay eat play)

10. The thirsty flowers began to **droop** in the hot sun.
(sag leaf drink)

11. Be careful you do not **wreck** the flower bed.
(help water ruin)

12. Our teacher is quite **cross** today.
(happy sad angry)

SIMILES

Similes are words used to compare people, animals or objects to something else. The words *as* and *like* are often used to make the comparison.

Example

Choose the best word from the brackets to fill the space.
*This baby lamb is as **playful** as a ________________.*
(kitten bone rock)
*Answer = This baby lamb is as **playful** as a **kitten**.*

Now do these the same way.

1. When she got a fright Linda went as **white** as a ________________.
   (box sheet table)

2. The spider's web was like a **maze** of ________________.
   (cotton insects spiders)

3. The sunset was as **red** as ________________.
   (fire clouds sky)

4. This glass of water is as **cold** as ________________.
   (ice fire wood)

5. My best friend John is **like** my ________________.
   (dog brother mate)

6. The grass was as **green** as ________________.
   (emeralds rubies cheese)

7. The Christmas tree looked like a **mass** of ________________.
   (jewels decorations angels)

8. Those stale lollies are now as **hard** as a ________________.
   (dove rock cup)

Now try making your own. You can use more than one word.

9. The fireworks looked like ________________________.

10. The fireworks were as loud as ________________________.

11. The squashed tomato was like ________________________.

12. The movie was as funny as ________________________.

UNIT 25 COMPOUND WORDS Year 5

Compound words are made up of two or more smaller words, joined together to make a new word.

Example

Write the word that best completes the sentence.
Dad cooked ***pan***_____________ *for my tea.*
(fill mill cakes)
Answer = Dad cooked ***pancakes*** *for my tea.*

Now do these the same way.
Some may have more than one correct answer.

1. I have finished my **home**_____________ at last.

2. At the beach I saw lots of **sea**_____________.

3. I put a **band**_____________ around his cut arm.

4. My **suit**_____________ was full of my old clothes.

5. The **sign**_____________ told me we still had ten kilometres to go.

6. I ordered a vanilla **milk**_____________ with my lunch.

7. We went for a long holiday on a **house**_____________.

8. I read all the recipes in the **cook**_____________.

9. It was so hot the children all had **sun**_____________.

10. The divers went down to explore the **ship**_____________.

11. We had to slow down because of the **road**_____________.

12. Fran put on her red **lip**_____________.

ANALOGIES

Just as a *young cat* is called a *kitten* so a *young sheep* is called a *lamb*. A similarity of this kind is called an analogy. An analogy shows how one thing is similar to something else.

Example

Add the word that best completes the analogy.
Dog is to puppy as cat is to ________________.
(lion kitten egg)
*Answer = **Dog** is to **puppy** as **cat** is to **kitten**.*

Now do these the same way.

1. **Up** is to **down** as **wet** is to ________________.
(hot dry old)

2. **Finger** is to **hand** as **toe** is to ________________.
(foot head heart)

3. **Spider** is to **fly** as **cat** is to ________________.
(dog mouse beetle)

4. **Gloves** are to **hands** as **shoes** are to ________________.
(shoulders arms feet)

5. **Father** is to **son** as **mother** is to ________________.
(uncle daughter cousin)

6. **Scales** are to **fish** as **feathers** are to ________________.
(dogs lions birds)

7. **June** is to **July** as **March** is to ________________.
(December April November)

8. **North** is to **south** as **east** is to ________________.
(west north backwards)

9. **Banana** is to **skin** as **orange** is to ________________.
(peel leaves juice)

10. **Sailor** is to **ship** as **pilot** is to ________________.
(car plane bike)

11. **Horse** is to **stable** as **dog** is to ________________.
(box kennel fence)

12. **Dog** is to **paw** as **horse** is to ________________.
(leg hoof page)

CONTRACTIONS

Contractions are made by joining two words together and leaving out a letter or letters. The missing letter/s are replaced by an apostrophe.

Contract the words in bold in the sentence.
*He **has not** got a clue.*
*Answer = He **hasn't** got a clue.*

Now try these. Write the contraction on the line.

1. **He has** got a new pushbike.

   ____

2. **He had** lost his old one.

   ____

3. He **could not** find it anywhere.

   ____

4. **He will** ride it to his friend's house.

   ____

5. **They will** take turns at riding it.

   ____

6. He **will not** leave his new bike unlocked.

   ____

7. **We are** going to the pool.

   ____

8. Do you know if **you are** going?

   ____

9. **There will** be lots of people there.

   ____

10. You **need not** take any lunch with you.

    ____

11. **We will** buy it at the kiosk.

    ____

12. If you **have not** got any money, **I will** shout you.

    ____

UNIT 28 ONE WORD FOR MANY Year 5

Sometimes we write a number of words when only one word would do just as well.

Example

What word could replace the bold words?
The jet is now ***able to be seen****.* ______________
(invisible gone visible)
Answer = The jet is ***visible****.*

Now do these the same way.

1. Stuart tripped and fell into the **small dirty pool**. ______________
(river puddle desert)

2. Ray had a **short sleep** after lunch.
____
(laugh nap game)

3. Diana **spoke in a quiet voice** to her friend. ______________
(whispered yelled jumped)

4. That story is **not true**.
____
(silly new false)

5. We will leave **in a short time**.
____
(soon never always)

6. Jan is sometimes **without manners**.
____
(stupid rude helpful)

7. If they do not find food they will **die of hunger**. ______________
(play chatter starve)

8. I paid the **money for the journey** to the conductor. ______________
(fair fare pager)

9. Mike is **unable to see**.
____
(deaf blind old)

10. My bedroom is **warm and comfortable.**
____
(untidy neat cosy)

11. I'm sure it was done **on purpose**.
____
(deliberately windy shabby)

12. I took **more than usual**.
____
(less extra none)

Most things around us can be placed in a certain class because they resemble other things, belong to the same family, or because of their purpose or use.

Example

Write the word that belongs in the same category.
rose daffodil tulip ________________
(beetle violet bush)
Answer = ***violet*** *because it is a flower, the same as roses, daffodils and tulips.*

Now do these the same way.

1. oats rice wheat ________________
(grass barley fruit)

2. beetle fly ant ________________
(cow insect bee)

3. dove plover emu ________________
(ostrich lion bird)

4. tennis hockey golf ________________
(cricket cards books)

5. violin piano harp ________________
(music guitar orchestra)

6. terrier collie greyhound
____
(animal spaniel hyena)

7. potato turnip carrot ________________
(beetroot tree apple)

8. yoghurt milk cheese ________________
(butter eggs cow)

9. hammer file screwdriver
____
(chisel mango tools)

10. sheet blanket mattress
____
(house bed pillow)

11. veal beef pork ________________
(bread fish bacon)

12. kitten calf puppy ________________
(bird foal eel)

Where do people or animals live? Where are things kept? Where do you buy things?

Example

Choose the correct place or thing.

You can buy flowers at a ________________

(greengrocer florist bakery)

Answer = You can buy flowers at a ***florist.***

Now do these the same way.

1. Cut flowers are kept in a ______________.
(blender vase kettle)

2. Stone for making roads is mined at a ________________.
(quarry carton theatre)

3. A doctor sees her patients in the ________________.
(bathroom bedroom surgery)

4. Beer is made at a __________________.
(garden brewery bakery)

5. Live fish are kept in an _____________________.
(igloo aquarium bath)

6. You can find lots of maps in an _________________.
(arena sty atlas)

7. Historical relics are displayed at a ________________.
(prison cafe museum)

8. Flour is ground from cereals at a ________________.
(house mill skyscraper)

9. Dead people are buried in a ________________.
(cemetery street bedroom)

10. Pet rabbits are kept in a ________________.
(box hutch bag)

11. Water is stored at a ________________.
(jar reservoir quarry)

12. Young plants and flowers are raised at a ________________.
(pantry nursery carton)

UNIT 31 PEOPLE AND OCCUPATIONS

What sort of person are you?

What occupation do you wish to follow when you finish your education?

Example

What occupation best fits the definition?
A person who sees the rules of a baseball match are obeyed is an ______________.
(soldier umpire pilot)
Answer = ***umpire***

Now do these the same way.

1. A person who eats too much is a ________________.
(glutton mutton painter)

2. A person living close by is your ________________.
(tailor neighbour dentist)

3. A person who carries your luggage is a ________________.
(umpire porter twin)

4. A person who sees an event take place is a ________________.
(daughter witness cleaner)

5. A person who investigates crime is a ________________.
(hero driver detective)

6. A person who moves cattle and sheep to market is a ________________.
(drover gypsy student)

7. A person who shoes horses is a ________________.
(captain mechanic farrier)

8. A person who carries a golfer's clubs is a ________________.
(cabbie caddy nurse)

9. A person who takes the money and checks out your groceries is a ________________.
(cleaner cashier mason)

10. A person who presides in a court of law is a ________________.
(judge drover sentry)

11. A trained cook in a hotel is called a ________________.
(porter chef waiter)

12. A person who studies the stars is an ________________.
(astronomer footballer cook)

Unit 1
1. nn 2. tt 3. bb
4. ss 5. tt 6. ss
7. rr 8. dd 9. ff
10. rr 11. ss 12. nn

Unit 2
1. knife 2. wrapper 3. hour
4. comb 5. calf 6. knee
7. sword 8. whole 9. climb
10. castle 11. palm 12. plumber

Unit 3
1. always 2. until 3. said
4. sugar 5. coming 6. beautiful
7. cotton 8. escape 9. awful
10. safety 11. forty 12. answer

Unit 4
1. craft 2. infant 3. allow
4. paint 5. repair 6. wand
7. teacher 8. lake 9. became
10. tractor 11. ready 12. sweep

Unit 5
1. its 2. full 3. walk
4. were 5. of 6. to
7. your 8. brought 9. adopt
10. lose 11. diary 12. does

Unit 6
1. carpenter 2. pyjamas 3. escaping
4. overhead 5. enjoyment 6. entertain
7. cabinet 8. develop 9. desperate
10. understand 11. Wednesday 12. companion

Unit 7
1. bl 2. cr 3. pl
4. cr 5. dr 6. br
7. sk 8. sm 9. pr
10. pl 11. pl 12. fr

Unit 8
1. mp 2. lt 3. sk
4. pt 5. st 6. mp
7. lp 8. ct 9. ft
10. lt 11. nd 12. ft

Unit 9
1. oi 2. ea 3. aw
4. ea 5. au 6. or
7. ey 8. oo 9. ei
10. dge 11. igh 12. ai

Unit 10
1. chief 2. thief 3. friend
4. piece 5. weight 6. spoonful
7. sweetly 8. easily 9. copying
10. angrily 11. hurrying 12. happiness

Unit 11
1. robbed 2. singing 3. stopped
4. watching 5. chasing 6. waving
7. hopeful 8. icing 9. dyeing
10. hopeless 11. trying 12. humming

Unit 12
1. trees 2. foxes 3. wishes
4. peaches 5. batches 6. ditches
7. glasses 8. brushes 9. potatoes
10. photos 11. volcanoes 12. radios

Unit 13
1. toys 2. donkeys 3. ponies
4. babies 5. calves 6. leaves
7. cliffs 8. handkerchiefs 9. shelves
10. teeth 11. men 12. children

Unit 14
1. little 2. butter 3. mother
4. yellow 5. forgot 6. swimming
7. church 8. birthday 9. pocket
10. asked 11. almost 12. people

Unit 15
1. un 2. un 3. il
4. un 5. un 6. im
7. in 8. un 9. dis
10. in 11. im 12. dis

Unit 16
1. en 2. able 3. est
4. ful 5. er 6. ness
7. ing 8. en 9. est
10. ful 11. er 12. ery

Unit 17
1. greater, greatest
2. cleaner, cleaned, cleanest, cleaning
3. sweeter, sweetest
4. seated, seating
5. presenter, presented, presenting
6. spooned, spoonful, spooning
7. flooded, flooding, floodable
8. flying, flyer, flyable
9. growing, grower, growable
10. kicked, kicking, kicker, kickable
11. informed, informing, informer, informant
12. dreamed, dreaming, dreamer

Unit 18
1. swim 2. crush 3. like
4. agree 5. finish 6. joy
7. health 8. build 9. like
10. complain 11. allow 12. fund

Unit 19
1. kitten rabbit 2. mother pillow 3. winter summer
4. forgot finger 5. monkey zebras 6. doctor button
7. people church 8. around circle 9. cheese dinner
10. donkey jumped 11. middle square 12. horses stables

Unit 20
1. lump 2. wasp 3. rose
4. lane 5. bowl 6. race
7. post 8. trap 9. how
10. table 11. march 12. steel

Unit 21
1. berry 2. bury 3. scent
4. grown 5. hour 6. our
7. lesson 8. lessen 9. missed
10. mist 11. pair 12. pour

Unit 22
1. awake 2. gentle 3. apart
4. plump 5. refuse 6. spend
7. filthy 8. backwards 9. outer
10. north 11. frown 12. feeble

Unit 23
1. brag 2. broad 3. fast
4. knock 5. own 6. garbage
7. border 8. warmth 9. decay
10. sag 11. ruin 12. angry

Unit 24
1. sheet 2. cotton 3. fire
4. ice 5. brother 6. emeralds
7. jewels 8. rock
9.–12. Answers will vary.

Unit 25
1. work 2. gulls or weed 3. age or aid
4. case 5. post 6. shake
7. boat 8. book
9. burn or stroke 10. wreck
11. works 12. stick

Unit 26
1. dry 2. foot 3. mouse
4. feet 5. daughter 6. birds
7. April 8. west 9. peel
10. plane 11. kennel 12. hoof

Unit 27
1. He's 2. He'd 3. couldn't
4. He'll 5. They'll 6. won't
7. We're 8. you're 9. There'll
10. needn't 11. We'll 12. haven't, I'll

Unit 28
1. puddle 2. nap 3. whispered
4. false 5. soon 6. rude
7. starve 8. fare 9. blind
10. cosy 11. deliberately 12. extra

Unit 29
1. barley 2. bee 3. ostrich
4. cricket 5. guitar 6. spaniel
7. beetroot 8. butter 9. chisel
10. pillow 11. bacon 12. foal

Unit 30
1. vase 2. quarry 3. surgery
4. brewery 5. aquarium 6. atlas
7. museum 8. mill 9. cemetery
10. hutch 11. reservoir 12. nursery

Unit 31
1. glutton 2. neighbour 3. porter
4. witness 5. detective 6. drover
7. farrier 8. caddy 9. cashier
10. judge 11. chef 12. astronomer

MASTERY TEST ANSWERS YEAR 5
1. ba**ll**oon 2. cas**t**le
3. almost 4. ack
5. loose 6. enjoyment
7. br 8. stand
9. boiling 10. field
11. swimming 12. churches
13. fairies 14. calendar
15. un 16. ful
17. present**ed** 18. open
19. purple, donkey 20. palm
21. team 22. hot
23. mistake 24. ice
25. fall 26. milk
27. I'll 28. blind
29. penguin 30. garage
31. police officer

Unit 1

1. ll	2. ll	3. ss
4. nn	5. dd	6. gg
7. gg	8. nn	9. ss
10. ll	11. rr	12. ff

Unit 2

1. limb	2. write	3. thistle
4. knob	5. island	6. answer
7. knitting	8. whistle	9. scissors
10. scent	11. science	12. doubt

Unit 3

1. address	2. destroy	3. burglar
4. almost	5. useful	6. film
7. athletes	8. library	9. hoping
10. woollen	11. surprise	12. separate

Unit 4

1. taste	2. prawn	3. match
4. feather	5. weight	6. early
7. brass	8. jacket	9. nerve
10. thief	11. tonight	12. desire

Unit 5

1. taught	2. dessert	3. breath
4. fuel	5. quite	6. too
7. loose	8. leant	9. drawers
10. already	11. hoarse	12. ladies

Unit 6

1. important	2. disaster	3. compartment
4. concluded	5. December	6. separate
7. exercises	8. invitation	9. education
10. occupation	11. electrical	12. punctuation

Unit 7

1. fl	2. gl	3. cr
4. dr	5. fl	6. cl
7. pr	8. fr	9. st
10. sp	11. tr	12. st

Unit 8

1. nd	2. nt	3. nd
4. sk	5. ct	6. ct
7. ft	8. nd	9. st
10 nd	11. pt	12. lt

Unit 9

1. ou	2. oo	3. ei
4. ou	5. ai	6. ar
7. ar	8. au	9. ea
10. ow	11. ue	12. ei

Unit 10

1. brief	2. niece	3. height
4. seized	5. receive	6. plentiful
7. thankful	8. carried	9. field
10. flying	11. trial	12. sleepily

Unit 11

1. planting	2. shopping	3. sinking
4. stabbed	5. tasting	6. ageless
7. chopping	8. priceless	9. scrubbed
10. shining	11. nicely	12. wasting

Unit 12

1. apples	2. boxes	3. beaches
4. crutches	5. mosses	6. gases
7. guesses	8. rushes	9. dingoes
10. mosquitoes	11. palms	12. shampoos

Unit 13

1. trolleys	2. storeys	3. injuries
4. countries	5. dictionaries	6. lives
7. cities	8. reefs	9. scarves
10. loaves	11. geese	12. lice

Unit 14

1. holiday	2. captain	3. bottom
4. welcome	5. pretty	6. evening
7. because	8. pencil	9. season
10. motor	11. saddle	12. juice

Unit 15

1. in	2. mis	3. non
4. dis	5. un	6. dis
7. un	8. un	9. im
10. im	11. dis	12. non

Unit 16

1. er	2. est	3. ful
4. ous	5. or	6. ness
7. ful	8. ting	9. ship
10. en	11. ish	12. less

Unit 17

1. preying, preyed
2. daring, darer, dared, dareable
3. caring, carer, cared, careable, careful
4. fearing, feared, fearful
5. clearing, clearer, cleared, clearest
6. delivering, deliverer, delivered, deliverable

7. watcher, watching watched, watchful
8. winder, winded, winding
9. teacher, teaching
10. harder, hardest
11. wounder, wounded, wounding
12. minder, minded, minding, mindful

Unit 18

1. employ 2. fresh 3. prison
4. advantage 5. plenty 6. angry
7. lucky 8. arm 9. circle
10. behave 11. appear 12. joint

Unit 19

1. family animal 2. season spring 3. twelve picnic
4. bottle bucket 5. couple church 6. bought orange
7. scream shadow 8. candle garage 9. answer doctor
10. collars calves 11. coffee mirror 12. saucer museum

Unit 20

1. same 2. leap 3. live
4. diet 5. thorn 6. never
7. clean 8. plate 9. team
10. blame 11. horse 12. taste

Unit 21

1. thrown 2. steal 3. prey
4. stake 5. through 6. waist
7. weather 8. pain 9. pier
10. guessed 11. scent 12. rowed

Unit 22

1. exit 2. beautiful 3. demolish
4. east 5. rare 6. heavy
7. gradual 8. broad 9. rude
10. sweet 11. solid 12. coarse

Unit 23

1. talk 2. tender 3. wrong
4. allow 5. damp 6. wash
7. copy 8. helper 9. fast
10. dizzy 11. bashful 12. sleepy

Unit 24

1. feather 2. soot 3. giraffe
4. rocks 5. teenager 6. lead
7. swan 8. cyclone
9.–12. Answers will vary.

Unit 25

1. quake 2. board 3. burger
4. fever 5. out 6. ache
7. glasses 8. ball 9. house
10. light 11. town 12. drums

Unit 26

1. fingers 2. pork 3. water
4. smell 5. princess 6. class
7. arrow 8. cub 9. fish
10. niece 11. book 12. pearls

Unit 27

1. mightn't 2. couldn't, he'll 3. you're
4. won't 5. I'd 6. it'll
7. They've 8. shouldn't 9. There'll
10. shouldn't 11. can't 12. haven't

Unit 28

1. century 2. culprit 3. antler
4. shattered 5. oval 6. drought
7. steam 8. cereal 9. timber
10. here 11. appetite 12. release

Unit 29

1. locust 2. spinach 3. sandal
4. surgeon 5. measles 6. bonnet
7. toaster 8. violet 9. bronze
10. cedar 11. skirt 12. opal

Unit 30

1. galah 2. yabby 3. merino
4. goanna 5. brumby 6. koala
7. joey 8. diggers 9. swaggie
10. bloke 11. taipan 12. emu

Unit 31

1. nappy 2. dressing gown 3. lollies
4. tap 5. rubbish 6. cupboard
7. holiday 8. timetable 9. petrol
10. soft-drink 11. car 12. tram

MASTERY TEST YEAR 6

1. gorilla 2. thistle
3. address 4. one
5. tried 6. disaster
7. pr 8. nd
9. stork 10. deceive
11. amazing 12. pianos
13. cities 14. picnic
15. un 16. dyeing
17. hopeful 18. prepare
19. stream, pretty 20. garden
21. through 22. drought
23. empty 24. ox
25. some 26. uncle
27. won't 28. oath
29. plane 30. budgerigar
31. cracker

[ ] denotes the unit to refer to.

1. Add the correct set of double letters. She blew up the ba _____oon. (rr ll mm) **[1]**
2. Circle the silent letter. castle **[2]**
3. Circle the correct spelling. It is (almost allmost) lunchtime. **[3]**
4. Circle the common letter pattern in each word. (back stack quack) **[4]**
5. Circle the correct word. The wheel has become (lose loose). **[5]**
6. Rearrange the syllables to make the word. (joy en ment) _______________ **[6]**
7. Add the correct initial blend. The door is _____oken. (pl br tr) **[7]**
8. Add the correct final blend. I am going to sta_____ here. (ft st nd) **[8]**
9. Add the correct sound unit. Is the water b_____ ling? (ar oi er) **[9]**
10. Choose the correct spelling: Thick grass grew in the (field feild). **[10]**
11. Choose the correct spelling. Mike is (swimming swiming). **[11]**
12. Make the word mean more than one. one church two __________ **[12]**
13. Make the word mean more than one. one fairy two __________ **[13]**
14. Circle the word that is spelt wrongly. I saw the date on the claender. **[14]**
15. Add the correct prefix. Scott is going to _____dress. (in un non) **[15]**
16. Add the correct suffix. We had better be care _____ (less ful) **[16,17]**
17. Add the correct suffix. He was present____ with a prize. (ing ed er) **[16,17]**
18. Circle the **base** word. **reopening** **[18]**
19. Make two words from the letters. (ple key pur don) colour __________ animal __________ **[19]**
20. Rearrange the word to fit the sentence. I climbed the __________ tree. (lamp) **[20]**
21. Choose the correct spelling. Rob is captain of our (team teem). **[21]**
22. Choose the opposite to the bold word. It is **chilly** in here. (cold hot silly) **[22]**
23. Choose the word that has the same meaning. Tom made an **error**. (pencil mistake plane) **[23]**
24. Add the best word. It is as cold as (fire ice water). **[24]**
25. Add the correct word. We swam near the water__________. (fall lake tea) **[25]**
26. Choose the best word. Tank is to water as carton is to __________. (milk salt chair) **[26]**
27. Contract the bold words. **I will** use a knife and fork. __________ **[27]**
28. Choose the word that could replace the bold words. The kittens are **unable to see**. (deaf blind happy) **[28]**
29. Add the word from the same group. dove magpie lark __________ (penguin horse bird) **[29]**
30. Choose the correct words. A car is kept in a __________. (tent garage bathroom) **[30]**
31. Choose the correct word. A person who upholds the law is a (doctor police officer dentist). **[31]**

UNIT 1 DOUBLE LETTERS Year 6

Double letters are an important part of many words we use everyday. They often occur naturally but sometimes have to be added when we add endings.
For example swim + ing = swimming

Write the correct double letters in the space.
I put a stamp on the le _____ er.
(rr tt ll)
*Answer = I put a stamp on the le**tt**er.*

Now do these the same way.

1. It was lucky the cars did not co_____ide at the corner.
(rr ll pp)

2. After I finish school I would like to go to co_____ege.
(pp tt ll)

3. Carrie was a pa_____enger on the train.
(ss mm nn)

4. The convicts dug a long tu_____el.
(nn rr gg)

5. You need a pa_____le to row a canoe.
(rr pp dd)

6. I found a small nu_____et of gold.
(pp gg rr)

7. We put all our lu_____age on the train.
(gg pp dd)

8. An Australian lizard is called a goa_____a.
(ll nn pp)

9. I used a compa_____ to find the direction I had to go.
(tt ss mm)

10. A large wi_____ow tree grew in the yard.
(ll tt rr)

11. A dried grape is called a cu_____ant.
(pp mm rr)

12. I like to eat a wa_____le with ice-cream.
(ff tt ll)

Silent letters were once sounded in the word. Although we no longer sound them we have left them in the original word. For this reason they can cause spelling difficulties.

Example

Write the correct word and circle the silent letter that fits the sentence.
We tied a __________ in the rope.
(knot loop)
Answer = We tied a **knot** in the rope.

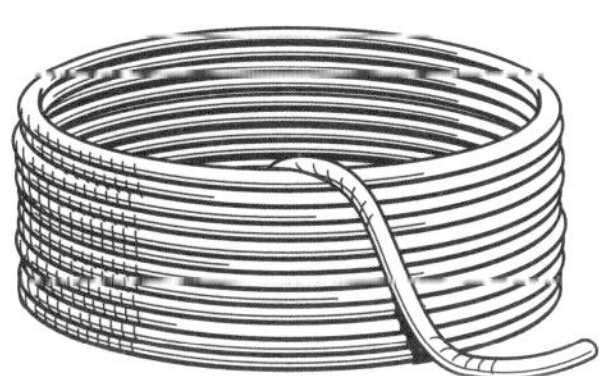

Now do these the same way.

1. An arm or leg is a __________ of your body.
(part limb)

2. I am going to __________ a story about dinosaurs.
(play write)

3. The sharp _______________ hurt his leg.
(thistle tree)

4. I broke the __________ on the door.
(handle knob)

5. The shipwrecked sailors swam to the nearby _______________.
(island waves)

6. What is the to question number five?
(answer desk)

7. Audrey is _______________ a jumper from that pretty, soft wool.
(playing knitting)

8. The umpire blew the _______________ to stop the game.
(trumpet whistle)

9. I cut the paper with a pair of _______________.
(scissors spoons)

10. The bloodhounds followed the __________ of the escaped convict.
(clothes scent)

11. My favourite school subject is _______________.
(playing science)

12. I __________ that Bill will be here before ten o'clock.
(doubt drink)

DEMON WORDS

Some words often cause us spelling difficulties. These words can be classed as Demon Words.

Example

Write the correct spelling of the word in the space.
When it is raining I always take my ______________.
(umberella umbrella)
Answer = When it is raining I always take my ***umbrella.***

Now do these the same way.

1. I wrote the ______________ on the envelope.
(adress address)

2. The strong wind may ______________ the crops.
(destroy distroy)

3. The ______________ was soon caught by the police.
(burgular burglar)

4. It is ______________ seven o'clock.
(allmost almost)

5. This is a very______________ gadget.
(useful usefull)

6. Last night we watched a ______________ about dinosaurs.
(filim film)

7. Billy and Alison are both very fine ______________.
(athletes athaletes)

8. There are lots of interesting books in the ______________.
(libary library)

9. We are all ______________ Kimberly wins the race.
(hopeing hoping)

10. This ______________ jumper is very warm.
(woolen woollen)

11. He got a big ______________ when he heard we had come.
(serprise surprise)

12. We took a long time to ______________ the fighting dogs.
(seperate separate)

UNIT 4 LETTER PATTERNS Year 6

There are letter patterns that occur frequently in many words. When trying to spell a word, try to think of a word that you know with the same pattern and it will help you to spell the new word.

Example

Circle the word which contains the same letter pattern as the bold word.
Write the pattern.
The train pulled into the ***station****.*
(library vacation taught)
Answer = ***ation***

Now do these. Write the word on the line and circle the pattern.

1. I stuck the paper on with some **paste.**
   ____
   (track splint taste)

2. We must leave at **dawn.**__________
   (glue prawn stew)

3. It is rude to **snatch** things from others.
   ____
   (beak match threat)

4. He dived under the water and held his **breath.** ______________
   feather spoon blown)

5. What is the **height** of that tower?
   ____
   (weight asleep repeat)

6. We went to bed early because we were **weary.** ______________
   (tired early silly)

7. We sat on the soft **grass.**
   ____
   (brass lawn crow)

8. I had a quick **snack** for lunch.
   ____
   (peach jacket lemon)

9. I feel you **deserve** a lot of credit for your work. __________
   (nerve liver desire)

10. The **chief** told us we could leave.
    ____
    (captain thief fire)

11. I got a **fright** when I saw the snake.
    ____
    (tonight blind yelled)

12. The **umpire** blew the whistle to stop the match. ______________
    (window witch desire)

UNIT 5 WORDS WE SOMETIMES CONFUSE Year 6

We often spell a word incorrectly because we confuse it with another word. This is particularly so for homophones (see Unit 21) and also for some other words.

Example

Write the correct word in the space.
The __________ ran across the paddock.
(horse hoarse)
Answer = The ***horse*** *ran across the paddock.*

Now do these the same way.

1. The coach_______________ me how to work the ball.
(taught learnt)

2. After the main course we had some _______________.
(desert dessert)

3. Tom dived under the water and held his _______________.
(breathe breath)

4. I filled the car up with _______________.
(fool fuel)

5. It is _______________ warm today.
(quiet quite)

6. It is far _______________ cold to go swimming today.
(to too two)

7. The nuts on the wheel began to work _______________.
(lose loose)

8. The farmer _______________ the shovel against the wall of the barn.
(leant learnt)

9. I put the ironed clothes inside the chest of _______________.
(draws drawers)

10. She was _______________ inside by the time we arrived.
(all ready already)

11. Her cold made her voice ____________.
(hoarse horse)

12. There are three _______________ in the room.
(ladys ladies)

UNIT 6 SYLLABLES Year 6

Every syllable contains a vowel sound. The vowels are a, e, i, o and u. Sometimes y is used as a vowel.

Rearrange the syllables and write the word in the space.
The lava flowed down the sides of the ______________.
(ca vol no)
Answer = The lava flowed down the sides of the ***volcano****.*

Now do these the same way.

1. It is ____________ we are not late for school today.
(ant im port)

2. The earthquake was a terrible ________________ for the city.
(ter dis as)

3. I hid the bottle in the small ________________ of the cupboard.
(ment part com)

4. We were glad the long speech was ________________.
(ded clu con)

5. The twelfth month of the year is ________________.
(ber cem De)

6. We had to ________________ the sugar from the salt.
(ate ar sep)

7. I like to do lots of physical ________________ at school.
(ex ci ses er)

8. I accepted his kind ________________.
(vi in tion ta)

9. It is important to get a good ________________.
(tion edu ca)

10. What is that lady's ________________?
(pa tion occ u)

11. The fire was caused by an ________________ fault.
(lec e al tric)

12. You must be careful with ________________ marks.
(tion punc a tu)

UNIT 7 INITIAL BLENDS Year 6

Many words begin with the same *initial* or starting blend of letters. It is important we recognise these and know the letters that come together to make the initial sound of the word.

Write the initial blend in the space.
The bony structure of your body is called your ____eleton.
(st sp sk)
Answer = The bony structure of your body is called your ***sk****eleton.*

Now do these the same way.

1. A large glass bottle is called a _____agon.
(dr fl br)

2. A river of ice is called a _____acier.
(br bl gl)

3. Plates, bowls and dishes are called _____ ockery.
(cr cl pr)

4. A period of dry weather is called a _____ought.
(br dr tr)

5. A large wading bird is a _____amingo.
(fr fl pl)

6. The weather conditions in a certain area are called the _____imate.
(cr br cl)

7. A wise old saying is called a ________overb.
(pr gr fr)

8. If you rub things together you create _____iction.
(fl fr br)

9. A male horse is called a _____allion.
(br st sc)

10. A small bird is a _____arrow.
(sl sp tr)

11. A stand with three legs is called a _____ipod.
(br tr gr)

12. The workers climbed up the _____eeple of the large cathedral.
(sc sp st)

FINAL BLENDS

Many words we use end in the same groups of letters. These letter groups are called *final blends*. It is important we are familiar with these.

Write the correct final blend in the space.
The farmer pulled the tree stu_____ out of the ground.
(st mp nt)
*Answer = The farmer pulled the tree stu**mp** out of the ground.*

Now do these the same way.

1. When iron is heated it will expa_____.
(st mt nd)

2. After the race the jockey began to dismou_____.
(st nt mt)

3. Jim is going to prete_____ he did his homework.
(nd st nt)

4. Simon carried a fla_____ of water in his pocket.
(sk nt lt)

5. The suspe_____ was arrested by the police.
(ct nd ct)

6. If you subtra_____ five from ten you get five.
(nd nt ct)

7. The horse chewed the tu_____ of grass.
(nd ft lt)

8. The stockmen are going to bra_____ the cattle.
(st nd mp)

9. That is the lea_____ amount of rain we have had for years.
(nd st mp)

10. The children began to dema_____ their rights.
(st nd mt)

11. Everyone exce_____ Leanne is allowed to come.
(sk pt lp)

12. The money is kept in this vau_____.
(nd lt lp)

SOUND UNITS

If we are to become good spellers we must know the different sounds made by individual letters or groups of letters.

Write the missing sound unit in the space.
A frog-like creature is called a t_____d.
(ea oa oo)
Answer = A frog-like creature is called a ***toad****.*

Now do these the same way.

1. A type of freshwater fish is a tr_____t.
(or ou er)

2. A bird that lays its eggs in other birds' nests is a cuck_____.
(oa oo ee)

3. The eagle s_____ zed the prey in its talons.
(ie ei or)

4. Iain wore his new tr_____sers to school.
(or ou an)

5. I thought it was a real barg_____n.
(ai ar ea)

6. The wine was kept in the cell_____.
(er ar ai)

7. A goanna is a large liz_____d.
(ue ar ea)

8. I put some tomato s_____ce on my pie.
(au or oo)

9. Summer is my favourite s_____son of the year.
(ee ea ai)

10. On a sunny day you can see your shad_____.
(ow ou or)

11. I stuck the paper together with gl_____.
(oo ue au)

12. This large truck carries fr_____ght to Melbourne.
(ie ei ea)

SPELLING RULES 1

Knowing certain spelling rules can help us become better spellers. However, to any rule there are exceptions so you must be on the look-out for these.

Rule 1 **-i** before **-e** except after **-c** when the sound is ee.
For example, **niece** **piece** but **ceiling**

However, **science**, **height**, **foreign** because the sound is not **-ee**.
When the sound is **-ay**, words are usually spelt **-ei** as in **neighbour**.

Rule 2 There is only one word that ends in **full** and that is the word **full** itself — all the others are **-ful**, for example, **beautiful**.

Rule 3 When a word ends in **-y** it is usually changed to **-i** when we add a suffix such as **-ly**, **-ful**, **-ed**. For example, **beauty** = **beautiful**.
It is not changed if we add **-ing** or we would have criing or hurriing.

Example

Put the correct spelling of the word in the space.
The dog is _________ the bone. (buriing burying)
Answer = The dog is ***burying*** *the bone.*

Now do these the same way.

1. The teacher gave us a _______________ lesson on road safety.
(breif brief)

2. Rebecca is my favourite ___________.
(neice niece)

3. What is the _______________ of that tower?
(hieght height)

4. The eagle _______________ the rabbit with its talons.
(siezed seized)

5. Did you _______________ my letter in the mail?
(recieve receive)

6. Ducks are _______________ at this time of year.
(plentiful plentifull)

7. I was _______________ she was not hurt.
(thanfull thankful)

8. I _______________ the baby to its cot.
(carryed carried)

9. I saw her in the _______________.
(field feild)

10. I can see a bird _______________ to its nest.
(flying fliing)

11. The _______________ of the thief took place last week.
(tryal trial)

12. She nodded her head _______________.
(sleepyly sleepily)

UNIT 11 SPELLING RULES 2 Year 6

Knowing certain spelling rules can help us become better spellers.

When a word ends in two consonants and we want to add **-ed** or **-ing** no letters are doubled. For example, **bang** becomes **banged** and **banging**

When a word ends in a consonant with one vowel before it we double the last letter before adding **-ed** or **-ing**. For example, beg – becomes **begged** or **begging**

When a word ends in a silent **-e** we drop the **-e** before adding **-ing**. For example, **shine – shining**. Exceptions include singeing, dyeing, canoeing, ageing.

If the suffix begins with a consonant the silent **-e** is usually retained.
For example, **care – careful**

Example

Write the correct spelling.
We went ______________ in the creek. (canoing canoeing)
Answer = We went ***canoeing*** *in the creek.*

Now do these the same way.

1. Tommy is _______________ a tree.
(planting plantting)

2. We are going _______________ this afternoon.
(shoping shopping)

3. The ship is _______________ beneath the water.
(sinking sinkking)

4. The man was _______________ in the leg.
(stabed stabbed)

5. I am _______________ the newly cooked food.
(tasteing tasting)

6. The legends I read about in this book are _______________.
(ageless agless)

7. Tim is _______________ the wood.
(choping chopping)

8. I thought the jokes he told were _______________.
(pricless priceless)

9. Con _______________ the kitchen floor.
(scrubed scrubbed)

10. The sun is _______________ brightly.
(shineing shining)

11. She spoke _______________ to the new pupil.
(nicely nicly)

12. Paul is _______________ his money again.
(wasteing wasting)

PLURALS 1

The word plural means more than one.

1. Most words simply add **-s** to form their plurals. For example, one **cat** — two **cats**
2. Words ending in **-ch, -s, -sh, -z** or **-x** add **-es** to make their plurals. For example, one **bush** — two **bushes**
3. Most words ending in **-o** add **-es** to make their plurals. For example, one **tomato** — two **tomatoes**. However some, like piano, kangaroo, bamboo, photo, boo, radio, banjo, just add **-s**.

Example

Write the plural in the space.
There are ten _______________ in this street. (house)
Answer = There are ten ***houses*** *in this street.*

Now do these the same way.

1. I ate three _______________ for lunch. (apple)
2. There are three _______________ on the table. (box)
3. There are lots of sandy _______________ in Australia. (beach)
4. Since he broke his leg Billy has to get around using_______________. (crutch)
5. There are some different types of _______________ growing on this rock. (moss)
6. Oxygen and nitrogen are two important _______________. (gas)
7. Tom made lots of _______________ before he got it correct. (guess)
8. There are lots of _______________ growing in the creek. (rush)
9. The three _____________ chased the sheep. (dingo)
10. All the _______________ spoiled our picnic. (mosquito)
11. There are lots of _______________ growing in our garden. (palm)
12. There are lots of different _______________ for your hair. (shampoo)

UNIT 13 PLURALS 2 Year 6

Plural means more than one. Some more plurals are:

1. Words ending in **vowel-y**, simply add **-s**. For example, one **monkey** — two **monkeys**
2. Words ending in **consonant-y** , change the **-y** to **-i** and add **-es**. For example, one **fairy** — two **fairies**
3. Words ending in **-f**, change the **-f** to **-v** and add **-es**. For example, one **wolf** — two **wolves**. However there are lots of exceptions. For example, one **chief** — two **chiefs**
4. Some words make their plurals by changing vowels or adding **-en**. For example, one **woman** — two **women** one **ox** — two **oxen**

Example

Write the plural.
I cut all the oranges into ______________. (half)
*Answer = I cut all the oranges into **halves**.*

Now do these the same way.

1. This supermarket has lots of ______________. (trolley)
2. This building is ten ______________ high. (storey)
3. The lady suffered lots of ______________ in the accident. (injury)
4. Mr Smith visited three foreign ______________ last year. (country)
5. Our classroom has two sets of ______________. (dictionary)
6. I read all about the ______________. of some famous people. (life)
7. Melbourne and Sydney are large ______________. (city)
8. The ship had to be careful not to get wrecked on one of the ______________. (reef)
9. Katya has lots of ______________ in the colours of her football team. (scarf)
10. The five ______________of bread are on the table. (loaf)
11. This farm has plenty of ______________. (goose)
12. The lady used a chemical to kill all the ______________ in the dog kennel. (louse)

UNIT 14 PROOFREADING Year 6

It is important that we are able to recognise whether a word is spelt correctly by simply looking at it. Proof reading is an important skill.

Example

In the sentence there is a word spelt incorrectly.
Write it correctly.
We are makeing some model aeroplanes. ______________
Answer = ***making***

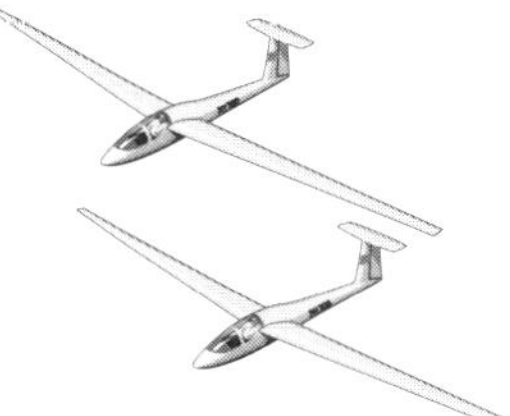

Now do these.

1. Next week we are going on an overseas holaday.

____

2. Rob is the captian of our football team.

____

3. We stayed at the bottum of the hill.

____

4. I am going to welcom the stranger to our school.

____

5. Emmy is a very pretti girl.

____

6. It was a nice evning to go walking.

____

7. Bill did not come becorse he was ill.

____

8. I draw a picture with my black pencill.

____

9. I always like the summer seeson.

____

10. The moter on the car is powered by petrol.

____

11. I put the saddel on the horse's back.

____

12. I drank a glass full of orange juce.

____

PREFIXES

Prefixes are syllables added to the front of a word. They are often used to change a word to its opposite meaning. When you add a prefix you do just that — no spelling changes are needed.

Example

Choose the correct prefix to make the word have an opposite meaning.
*This is a _____**fiction** book about monkeys. (un non il)*
*Answer = This is a **nonfiction** book about monkeys.*

Now do these the same way.

1. The answer Billy gave was _____**correct.** (un in mis)

2. I have _____**placed** my pencil. (un mis ir)

3. This is a _____**smoking** area. (un mis non)

4. I saw the plane _____**appear** into the clouds. (dis mis il)

5. The drunken man was _____**steady** on his feet. (mis un in)

6. I _____**like** eating turnips and carrots. (un dis im)

7. Paul is very _____**popular** because he is selfish. (un dis mis)

8. The story I heard is _____**true**. (in un il)

9. It is _____**possible** for Harry to jump over that fence. (im il non)

10. Neil is a very _____**mature** boy. (il im in)

11. Kim will probably _____**obey** the teacher again. (dis un mis)

12. This is a silly story: it is really all just _____**sense**. (non im dis)

SUFFIXES

Suffixes are groups of letters added to the ends of words to build new words.

Example

Add the correct suffix from the brackets to complete the word.
Mr Jones is a famous ***art*** *_____. (ish ist)*
*Answer = Mr Jones is a famous art****ist****.*

Now do these the same way.

1. This table is **light**_____ than that one.
(or er)

2. This is the **long**_____ way to go.
(est ful)

3. The room was a **disgrace**_____ mess.
(less ful)

4. A taipan is a very **danger**_____ snake.
(ous ure)

5. My uncle is a famous **act**_____.
(er or)

6. I appreciated her **kind**_____.
(ness est)

7. I thought that was a **dread**_____ thing to do.
(ful ible)

8. My grandmother is **knitt**_____ me a jumper.
(er ing)

9. The two men faced a lot of **hard**_____ together.
(ship sure)

10. We are going to **dark**_____ the room.
(er en)

11. That was a very **fool**_____ thing to do.
(ish less)

12. This forged money is **worth**_____.
(ire less)

Example

Using the suffixes in the box, see how many new words you can build.

ed	ing	er
able	ful	est

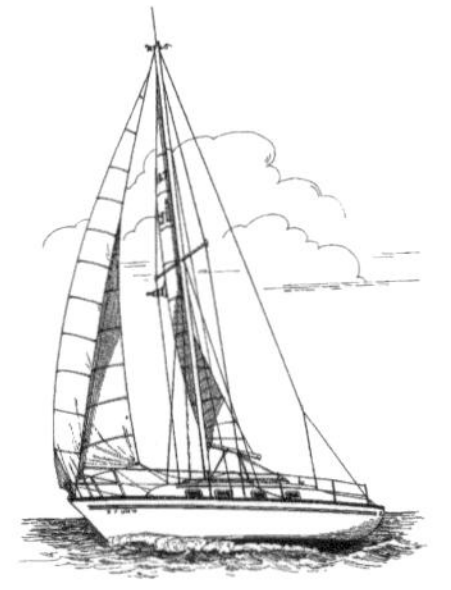

Base word = sail
Answer = sailing, sailed, sailable.

Now try these.

ing	er	ed
able	ful	est

1. prey ______________________________
____

2. dare ______________________________
____

3. care______________________________
____

4. fear ______________________________
____

5. clear ______________________________
____

6. deliver ______________________________
____

er	ed	ing
ance	est	ful

7. watch ______________________________
____

8. wind ______________________________
____

9. teach ______________________________
____

10. hard ______________________________

11. wound ______________________________
____

12. mind ______________________________
____

UNIT 18 BASE WORDS Year 6

From *base* words we can build other words by adding a *prefix* or a *suffix* or *both*. For example:

Base Word	Add Prefix	Add Suffix
lock	**un**lock	**un**lock**ed**
happy	**un**happy	**un**happi**ness**
appear	**dis**appear	**dis**appear**ed**

Sometimes the base word may be hard to see because of spelling changes. For example, **happiness** — base word is **happy**.

Example

Write the **base** word from which the bold word comes.
There are a lot of goods still ***unclaimed.*** ________________
Answer = ***claim***

Now do these the same way. Circle the suffix or prefix and write the base word on the line.

1. My father has been **unemployed** for two years.

   ____

2. At the station we had some **refreshments.**

   ____

3. The thief was sentenced to two years **imprisonment.**

   ____

4. If we stay here we are at a **disadvantage.**

   ____

5. Mushrooms are **plentiful** this year.

   ____

6. His behaviour made me **angrier** than I've ever been.

   ____

7. I think I am the **luckiest** student in the school.

   ____

8. The police soon **disarmed** the men.

   ____

9. The pelicans **encircled** the fish.

   ____

10. Tommy could not go to play because he **misbehaved** in class.

    ____

11. The comet will be **reappearing** next year.

    ____

12. It seems that this story is quite **disjointed**.

    ____

MAKING WORDS

It is important for us to recognise the letter pieces that make up a word.

Example

Join the letter pieces together to make words that match the sentence.

This ______________ is very ______________.

(row nar der lad)

Answer = This ***ladder*** *is very* ***narrow****.*

Now do these.

1. Our ______________ found a strange ______________ in the bush.
(mal fam ani ily)

2. My favourite ______________ of the year is ______________.
(spr sea ing son)

3. There were ______________ children at the ______________.
(lve pic twe nic)

4. I filled a ______________ and a ______________with water.
(bot buc tle ket)

5. The ______________ will marry in the ______________ next Saturday.
(rch ple cou chu)

6. I ______________ an ______________ for my lunch.
(ght nge ora bou)

7. The boy began to ______________ when he saw the ______________.
(dow scr sha eam)

8. I lit a ______________in the dark ______________.
(age can gar dle)

9. What ______________ did the ______________ give you?
(tor wer doc ans)

10. I put ______________ on the ______________.
(col ves cal lars)

11. I drank a cup of ______________ as I stood in front of the ______________.
(fee ror mir cof)

12. I gave the old ______________ I found to the curator of the ______________.
(eum cer mus sau)

ANAGRAMS

Anagrams are words we can make by rearranging the letters of another word.

Example

Rearrange the letters to make a word that fits the sentence.
Your ________________ pumps blood around your body.
(earth)
Answer = Your ***heart*** *pumps blood around your body.*

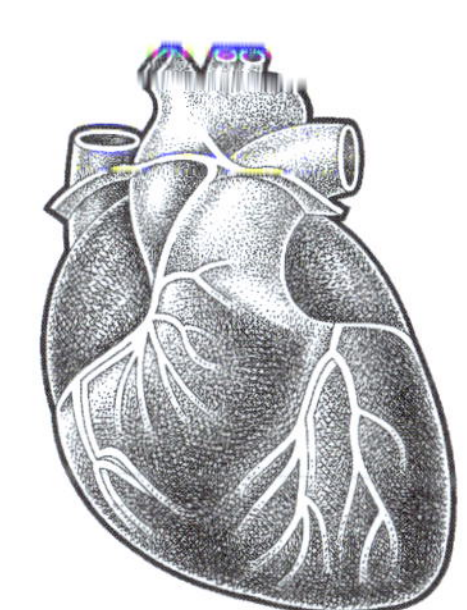

Now do these the same way.

1. My football is exactly the ________________ as yours.
(seam)

2. We saw the kangaroo ________________ over the fence.
(peal)

3. How long does a butterfly ________________?
(evil)

4. I have been eating too much so I am going on a ________________.
(edit)

5. A large ________________ was stuck in the dog's paw.
(north)

6. "I have ________________ been here before," said Tom.
(nerve)

7. The dirty socks are now ________________.
(lance)

8. I put the food on the ________________.
(petal)

9. John is the captain of our ________________.
(meat)

10. Everyone tried to ________________ Bill for our team losing the match.
(amble)

11. I rode the ________________ along the road.
(shore)

12. A lemon has a bitter ________________.
(state)

HOMOPHONES

Homophones are words that sound the same but have different spellings and different meanings. For this reason it is important we know both the spelling and the meaning of these words.

Example

Write the correct word.
There are seven days in a ________________.
(week weak)
Answer = There are seven days in a ***week.***

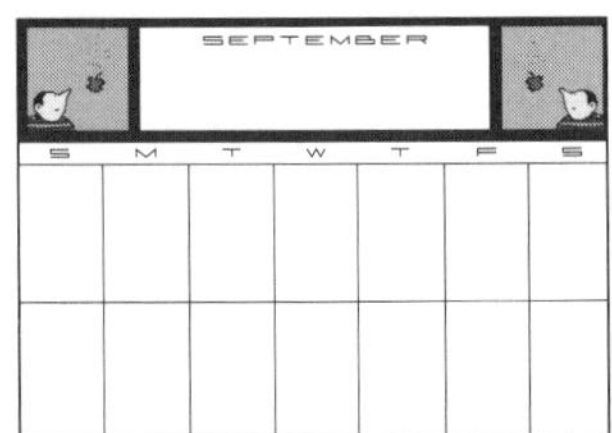

Now do these the same way.

1. In the fight, a chair was ________________ across the room.
(throne thrown)

2. The thieves tried to ________________ the jewels.
(steal steel)

3. The eagle clasped its ________________ in its powerful talons.
(pray prey)

4. I hammered the ________________ into the ground.
(stake steak)

5. The children ran ________________ the corridors.
(threw through)

6. Lise wore a black belt around her ________________.
(waist waste)

7. The ________________ has been very cold lately.
(whether weather)

8. Caleb has a severe ________________ in his leg.
(pane pain)

9. We walked along the ________________.
(peer pier)

10. I am sure Josh ________________ the right answer.
(guest guessed)

11. This ________________ has a very sweet smell.
(sent cent scent)

12. The boys ________________ the boat across the lake.
(road rowed rode)

ANTONYMS

Antonyms are words that have opposite, or nearly opposite, meanings.

Example

Choose the word with the opposite meaning.
That towel is wet but this one is ______________.
(old dry blue)
*Answer = That towel is **wet** but this one is **dry**.*

Now do these the same way.

1. Here is the **entrance** to the building and there is the ______________.
(door exit office)

2. That butterfly is **ugly** but this one is quite ______________.
(beautiful common false)

3. We are going to **build** a house here and ______________ that one.
(demolish forget attack)

4. Some people walked **west** while the others walked ______________.
(south east north)

5. Those beetles are **common** but these are quite ______________.
(dry rare far)

6. That table is **light** but these are very ______________.
(solid heavy green)

7. Instead of a **sudden** movement you should make a ______________ one.
(gradual hairy noisy)

8. This laneway is **narrow** while that one is______________.
(thin broad flat)

9. Ian is always **polite** but David is often ______________.
(quiet rude bright)

10. That lolly is **bitter** but this one is ______________.
(new sweet dirty)

11. That log is **hollow** but this one is ______________.
(round solid loose)

12. That paper is **smooth** but this lot is ______________.
(common scarce coarse)

SYNONYMS

Synonyms are words that have the same, or nearly the same, meaning.

Circle the word that has the same meaning as the bold word.
*Do you think we will be able to **locate** the treasure?*
(lose find steal)
*Answer = **find***

Now, circle the word which has the same, or nearly the same, meaning.

1. After the fight the boys began to **speak** again.
   (race talk play)

2. This cut of meat is quite **soft**.
   (old hard tender)

3. His answer was **incorrect.**
   (right wrong stupid)

4. My parents said they would **let** me go to the disco.
   (help allow aloud)

5. This piece of cloth is quite **moist**.
   (damp dry coloured)

6. I began to **launder** the dirty clothes.
   (sew toss wash)

7. Did you see the monkey **imitate** the keeper?
   (copy bite grab)

8. Peter is going to be the teacher's **assistant** today.
   (pet helper father)

9. His heartbeat became **very rapid**.
   (slow fast bumpy)

10. After the illness she was quite **giddy**.
    (weak dizzy happy)

11. Cath is quite a **shy** girl.
    (cheeky bashful tall)

12. I am starting to feel **drowsy.**
    (sleepy ill peculiar)

SIMILES

Similes are words used to compare people, animals or objects to something else. The words *as* and *like* are often used to make the comparison.

Example

Choose the best word from the brackets to fill the space in the sentence.
My exam results were like a dream come ________________.
(true awake asleep)
Answer = My exam results were like a dream come ***true****.*

Now do these the same way.

1. This new material is as light as a ________________.
(rock sheep feather)

2. The sky was as black as ________________.
(soot rain rats)

3. My friend Joe is as tall as a ______________.
(giraffe cow shed)

4. These old lollipops are as hard as ______________.
(wool rocks paper)

5. Although he is over eighty years old Mr Wong is still as fit as a ________________.
(teenager pig tree)

6. These things we have to lift are as heavy as ________________.
(lead snow feathers)

7. When she dances Sue is as graceful as a ________________.
(swan feather mouse)

8. The old shed looked like it had been hit by a ________________.
(fire cyclone rocket)

Now try making up your own. You can use more than one word.

9. The newborn foal was as wobbly as ____________________________.

10. The sunset looked like ____________________________.

11. My new haircut was ____________________________.

12. My friend's new skateboard is ____________________________.

COMPOUND WORDS

Compound words are made up of two or more smaller words, joined together to make a new word.

Example

Write the word that best completes the sentence.
Dad cooked ***pan*** *_______________ for tea.*
Answer = Dad cooked ***pancakes*** *for tea.*

Now do these the same way.
Some may have more than one possible answer.

1. A violent **earth**_____________ shook the city.

2. Tom brought his new **skate**_____________ to school.

3. Phil ate a **cheese**_____________ for lunch.

4. Every spring I get a bad dose of **hay**_____________.

5. At the top of the mountain there was a **look**_____________.

6. Clare isn't feeling well because she has a **tooth**_____________.

7. The film star wore some **sun**__________.

8. Are you going to play **volley**_____________ tonight?

9. The judge ordered the people out of the **court**_____________.

10. We could see the trees in the bright **moon**_____________.

11. We are going **down** _____________ after school.

12. The loud noise nearly burst her **ear**_____________.

UNIT 26 ANALOGIES Year 6

Just as a *young cat* is called a *kitten* so a *young sheep* is called a *lamb*. A similarity of this kind is called an analogy. An analogy shows how one thing is similar to something else.

Example

Add the word that best completes the analogy.
Mother is to baby as cow is to ______________.
(child calf egg)
*Answer = **Mother** is to **baby** as **cow** is to **calf**.*

Now do these in the same way.

1. **Foot** is to **toe** as **hand** is to ______________.
(mouth teeth fingers)

2. **Sheep** is to **mutton** as **pig** is to ________.
(fish pork wheat)

3. **Aeroplane** is to **air** as **ship** is to ______________.
(wood water land)

4. **Eye** is to **sight** as **nose** is to ______________.
(feel smell taste)

5. **Mother** is to **daughter** as **queen** is to ______________.
(prince king princess)

6. **Footballer** is to **team** as **student** is to ______________.
(class pencils seats)

7. **Rifle** is to **bullet** as **bow** is to ______________.
(rocket arrow spear)

8. **Dog** is to **puppy** as **bear** is to ______________.
(kitten cub foal)

9. **Wing** is to **bird** as **fin** is to ______________.
(dog fish spider)

10. **Uncle** is to **nephew** as **aunt** is to ______________.
(cousin niece daughter)

11. **Artist** is to **painting** as **author** is to ______________.
(vase book oranges)

12. **Flock** is to **sheep** as **string** is to ______________.
(pearls toes matches)

CONTRACTIONS

Contractions are made by joining two words together and leaving a letter or letters out. The missing letter/s are replaced by an apostrophe.

Example

Contract the words in bold in the sentence.
We will *have a barbecue on Sunday.*
Answer = ***We'll*** *have a barbecue on Sunday.*

Now try these. Write the contraction on the line.

1. Jim **might not** be able to come to the party.

   ____

2. He said if he **could not he will** ring you.

   ____________, ____________

3. Do you know if **you are** able to go?

   ____

4. I **will not** know till Thursday.

   ____

5. If I can **I had** better buy a present.

   ____

6. I think **it will** be good fun.

   ____

7. **They have** been caught cheating in their exam.

   ____

8. They **should not** have done that.

   ____

9. **There will** be a lot of trouble when their parents find out.

   ____

10. I **should not** be surprised if they get suspended.

    ____

11. They **cannot** expect to be treated lightly.

    ____

12. I **have not** a clue why they did it.

    ____

ONE WORD FOR MANY

Sometimes we write a number of words when only one word would do just as well.

Example

What word could replace the bold words?
We put the ***water that is solid*** *in the glass.* ____________
(liquid hard ice)
Answer = We put the ***ice*** *in the glass.*

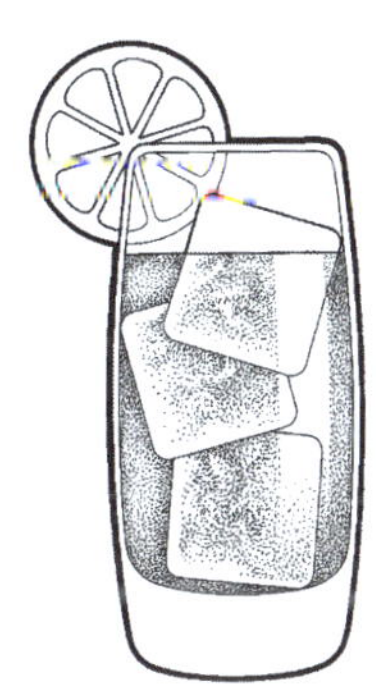

Now do these the same way.

1. The town is a **hundred years** old.
____
(decade century cosy)

2. The **guilty person** was soon caught by the police. ____________
(culprit teacher child)

3. He hung the **horn of the deer** on the wall.
____
(moose hoof antler)

4. The glass was **broken into pieces**.
____
(shifted shattered joined)

5. This cricket ground is **shaped like an egg**.
____
(square oval green)

6. A **long dry period** destroyed the crops.
____
(drought cloud desert)

7. The **water that is gas** burnt my hand.
____
(steam train ice)

8. I put the **food made from grain** in the bowl.
____
(serial cereal tomatoes)

9. The **wood for building** is in the yard.
____
(tree timber plastic)

10. Jeannie put the box **in this place**.
____
(here soon under)

11. I have lost my **desire for food**.
____
(eggs appetite hamburger)

12. We decided to **let** the rabbit **go**.
____
(hold release start)

Most things around us can be placed in a certain class because they resemble other things, belong to the same family, or because of their purpose or use.

Example

Write the word that belongs to the same class.
sloop boat dinghy ______________
(car yacht truck)
Answer = ***yacht*** *because it is a sailing vessel, the same as sloops, boats and dinghies.*

Now do these the same way.

1. mosquito moth beetle
____
(locust tractor apricot)

2. cabbage cauliflower celery
____
(towel mango spinach)

3. boot shoe thong ______________
(tie collar sandal)

4. physician patient nurse
____
(surgeon mechanic teacher)

5. fever arthritis mumps
____
(games baldness measles)

6. hat beret helmet
____
(belt bonnet sleeve)

7. blender mincer grater
____
(toaster book table)

8. rose daffodil tulip
____
(beetle violet bush)

9. brass copper gold ______________
(wool glass bronze)

10. eucalyptus palm poplar
____
(cedar table lemonade)

11. cardigan jumper coat
____
(curtain cushion skirt)

12. diamond emerald ruby
____
(opal watch bracelet)

UNIT 30 AUSTRALIAN WORDS Year 6

Did you know that many of the words we use every day originated in Australia? We have our own special words for many of the things around us.

Example

What word best describes the thing in the sentence?
A wild dog of Australia is called a ________________.
(billy dingo postie)
Answer = A wild dog of Australia is called a ***dingo****.*

Now do these.

1. A pink and grey Australian cockatoo is called a ________________.
(galah reptile)

2. A small Australian crayfish is called a ________________.
(crab yabby)

3. A sheep that is famous for its fine wool is a ________________.
(jersey merino)

4. A large Australian lizard is a ________________.
(gecko goanna)

5. The name given to a wild horse is a ________________.
(brumby cocky)

6. The name given to the small bear-like marsupial is a ________________.
(rosella koala)

7. The name we give to a baby kangaroo is a ________________.
(billy joey)

8. The name given to Australian soldiers is ________________.
(diggers cockies)

9. A person who once roamed the country was called a ________________.
(cabbie swaggie)

10. The name given to a male is a ________________.
(bloke mossie)

11. A very venomous Australian snake is a ________________.
(taipan tarantula)

12. A very large Australian bird that cannot fly is an ________________.
(budgerigar emu)

AMERICAN WORDS

Although English is spoken by people from the United States of America, many of their words differ in meaning to ours.

Example

Choose our word for the bold American word.
*I ate a **cookie** after tea.* ________________
(meatball biscuit lolly)
Answer = ***biscuit***

Now do these the same way.

1. The mother put the clean **diaper** on the baby. ________________
(bib bonnet nappy)

2. Before I went to bed I put on my **robe**. ________________
(tie dressing gown boot)

3. Do you want some more **candy**?
____
(pencils water lollies)

4. I turned on the **faucet**. ________________
(electricity tap television)

5. The **trash** was taken out of the room.
____
(chains rubbish money)

6. I put the goods in the **closet**.
____
(cupboard box basket)

7. I have just returned from my **vacation**.
____
(house holiday occupation)

8. The teacher pinned the **schedule** on the board. ________________
(timetable team jumper)

9. We put some **gasoline** in the car.
____
(petrol grease air)

10. I asked for a bottle of **soda**.____________
(salt soft drink detergent)

11. My father has a new **automobile.**
____
(tractor car bicycle)

12. I caught the **streetcar** to go to the party.
____
(taxi bus tram)

MASTERY TEST Year 6

[ ] **denotes the unit to refer to.**

1. Add the set of double letters. We saw the gori_____a at the zoo. (pp rr ll) **[1]**
2. Circle the silent letter in thistle. **[2]**
3. Circle the correct spelling of the word. I wrote the_____ on the envelope. (adress address adres) **[3]**
4. Circle the common letter pattern. honey money cone **[4]**
5. Circle the correct word. I (tried tied) to do better. **[5]**
6. Rearrange the syllables to make the word. The earthquake was a great (as dis ter). _____________ **[6]**
7. Add the correct initial bend. Who is the _____incipal of the school? (br st pr) **[7]**
8. Add the correct final blend. When it is hot steel will expa_____. (st nd lp) **[8]**
9. Add the correct sound unit. A type of bird is a st_____k. (ar ai or). [9]
10. Circle the correct spelling of the word. (deceive decieve) **[10]**
11. Choose the correct spelling of the word. I found it _____. (amazeing amazing) **[11]**
12. Make this word mean more than one. one **piano** two _________ **[12]**
13. Make this word mean more than one. one **city** two _________ **[13]**
14. Circle the word that is spelt incorrectly. We went on a picnick yesterday. **[14]**
15. Add the correct prefix to make the opposite meaning. The paper has become ____**stuck**. (in un im) **[15]**
16. Add the correct suffix. We are dye_____ the cloth. (ing ful) **[16/17]**
17. Add the correct suffix. We are very hope____ about the result. (les ful) **[16/17]**
18. Circle the **base** word from which this word is formed. **unprepared** **[18]**
19. Join the word parts to make two words that match the meanings. (eam str tty pre) river _________ not ugly _________ **[19]**
20. Rearrange the letters to make a word that fits the sentence. Some roses grew in the _________. (danger) **[20]**
21. Circle the correct word in the brackets. We ran (threw through) the room. **[21]**
22. Circle the opposite of the bold word. There was a **flood** last year. (rain drought cloud) **[22]**
23. Circle the word that means the same as the bold word. The building is **vacant**. (old empty drab) **[23]**
24. Choose the word that completes the sentence. John is a strong as an (apple ox deer) **[24]**
25. Add the best word to complete the compound word. Bill is a hand_____ boy. (with some break) **[25]**
26. Choose the best word to complete the sentence. Niece is to nephew as aunt is to _____. (cousin uncle brother) **[26]**
27. Contract the words in bold. We **will not** be going tomorrow. _________ **[27]**
28. Choose the one word that could replace the bold words. I gave her a **solemn promise**. (oath pencil lie) **[28]**
29. Circle the word that goes with the first group. scissors pliers hammer (table plane road) **[29]**
30. Which word means a small parrot? (gecko budgerigar yabby) **[30]**
31. Which word means a dry biscuit? (muffin bulletin cracker) **[31]**

Notes